To the MKs.

Foreword

by Ruth E. Van Reken

I WISH I'D SEEN THIS BOOK WHEN I WAS THIRTEEN. That's the year I permanently retuned "home"—to the U.S., that is—after having spent my life as a missionary kid (MK) in Nigeria.

Thirteen probably isn't anyone's best age, but for me it was particularly stressful. I finally figured out I must be the only person alive that hadn't heard of Elvis, never remembered that the price marked on a product didn't include something called tax, and thought my donated saddle shoes were the height of fashion. Everyone else could ice skate with ease, while my wobbly ankles barely held me up on those thin blades for thirty seconds before an inglorious fall on the ice. Why was I always so different?

Of course, there were wonderful moments, too. A new chain with golden arches had just begun. Kind American friends gave us all sorts of treats. I gained thirty pounds in three months while enjoying every bite of newly discovered McDonald's hamburgers and fries (with a chocolate shake on the side, of course), real ice cream of countless flavors, unlimited Coke, and seconds or thirds on meat that could be chewed without pressure cooking it.

But the hardest part of that year was the growing sense that something must be wrong with me. Why was I always so "out-of-sync" with others? I felt sure no one else could have felt this awkward or ignorant or full before. It never occurred to me how different my past experiences had been from these, my fellow citizens and peers. It probably never occurred to them, either. All I knew, and likely all they knew, was that Ruth seemed a little "odd."

That's why I wish I could have read *You Know You're an MK When...* right about then.

There is a special joy that comes to all of us when we suddenly realize that in the secret place where we felt that no one else could possibly understand us, we're wrong. Someone else does know—and if someone else knows what we feel, then we're no longer alone.

That's the joy of reading this booklet. The recognition that almost catches us off guard when we realize someone has put words on a thought, feeling, or action we considered uniquely our own makes us want to laugh—or cry.

I laughed when I read that you know you're an MK when you send Kool-Aid and peanut butter in a package. For years, friends who visited our home at Christmas unwrapped soap, candy bars, and even toothpaste as part of their "extra gifts." I've always wondered at their slightly befuddled looks as they strive to respond with appropriate appreciation and realized as I read this statement that maybe other people don't usually give such gifts! It's been so much a part of my missionary subculture and life-style that it seemed normal.

As a child, I would have been disappointed not to get Cokes and candy bars from my siblings because I didn't have the money to buy them easily myself.

Reading this booklet, I felt amazement. So someone else had problems with the sorry word too! I'm not crazy after all. For years, although I could never understand it, I accepted my friend's judgment that I didn't feel good if I didn't feel guilty—all because I said "sorry" for everything. It tool me a long time to understand that saying sorry in the States implies an apology for something a person does rather than expressing sympathy as it does in all other languages I've learned.

The list made me squirm, as well. It hit those old "I'll never get it all right" buttons. Now I wonder what my gracious hostesses in Australia really think of me after I did manage to finish my generously loaded plates (#42 and #43). The last thing I wanted was for them to think I disliked their luscious food—even though it cost me several pounds in weight. In my struggle to finish the food, it never occurred to me that maybe I wasn't supposed to!

And, as an MK, I read some of these statements reflecting thoughts I admit I've had and felt a bit rebuked—rebuked by the reflection that sometimes I've been willing to validate every culture but my own. In the effort to acknowledge and affirm the rich gifts of my past, it's easy to put others down and do to others what I'd rather they didn't do to me.

But it is this representation of the wide range of common MK experiences which makes *YKYAMKW* such a fun—and useful—book. Andy and Deborah have collected these snippets from MKs all over the world. While the specific examples in each statement reflect the many cultural backgrounds in which these MKs were raised, the feelings here transcend the specifics. All who read this—MKs or not—will gain a deeper understanding of the experiences and feelings many MKs and other cross-cultural sojourners as children have known.

Thanks to my friends on the MKnet and MK-Issues who sent in so many fun, and useful, insights. And thanks, Andy and Deborah, for the service you have done us all in compiling this book. It's a great tool to help MKs and adult MKs everywhere put better words on our life experience, and give us all a fun way to share it with others.

Ruth E. Van Reken

Ruth is a free-lance writer and speaker whose various works include Letters Never Sent—*an account of her own MK journey. She has also written a chapter on "Religious Culture Shock" for* Strangers at Home *(Aletheia Press). Her latest book,* Third Culture Kids, The Experience of Growing Up Among Worlds, *is co-authored with David C. Pollock and is published by Nicholas Brealey Publishing/Intercultural Press. She can be contacted at Box 90084, Indianapolis, IN 46290–0084, by telephone or fax (317) 251–4933 or e-mail at RDVanreken@aol.com.*

You Know You're an MK when...

1.   You can't answer the question, "Where are you from?"

2.   You have a trunk for a coffee table, and think that barrels make good night stands.

3.   The vast majority of your clothes are hand-me-downs.

4.   People send you used tea bags in the mail.

5.   You speak two languages, but can't spell in either.

You Know You're an MK when...

6. You flew before you could walk.

7. The US is a foreign country.

8. You embarrass yourself by asking what swear words mean.

9. You have a passport, but no driver's license.

10. You watch National Geographic specials and recognize someone.

11. You don't know how to play Pac-Man.

12. You have a time zone map next to your telephone.

13. You consider a city 500 miles away to be "very close."

14. Your life story uses the phrase "Then we went to..." five times.

15. You prefer a Land Rover to a Lambourghini.

16. National Geographic makes you homesick.

You Know You're an MK when...

17. You can cut grass with a machete, but can't start a lawn mower.

18. You think in grams, meters, and liters.

19. You speak with authority on the subject of airline travel.

20. You go to the US, and get sick from a mosquito bite.

21. You send your family peanut butter and Kool-Aid for Christmas.

You Know You're an MK when...

22. You worry about fitting in, and wear a native wrap around the dorm.

23. You watch nature documentaries, and you think about how good that animal or insect would be if it were fried.

24. You have strong opinions about how to cook bugs.

25. You turn to the international section of the paper before the comics.

26. You live at school, work in the tropics, and go home for vacation.

27. Your eggs are delivered to you—from a plane flying at 2000 feet.

28. Strangers say they can remember you when you were "This tall."

29. You grew up with a maid.

30. You do your devotions in another language.

You Know You're an MK when...

31. You sort your friends by continent.

32. You keep dreaming of a green Christmas.

33. 011 is a familiar area code.

34. You see bread made with caraway seeds, and think the flour had weevils in it.

35. The nationals say, "Oh, I knew an American once..." and then ask if you know him or her.

36. You aren't terribly surprised when you do.

37. You are grateful for the speed and efficiency of the US Postal Service.

38. You realize that furlough is not a vacation.

39. You'd rather never say hello than have to say good-bye.

40. You wince when people mispronounce foreign words.

41. You've spoken in dozens of churches, but aren't a pastor.

42. Furlough means that you are stuffed every night... and have to eat it all to seem polite.

43. You realize that in Australia, statement 42 would be very rude.

44. You commit verbal faux pas, as demonstrated in statement 43.

45. Your parents decline your cousin's offer to let them use his BMW, and shoehorn all six of you into an old VW Beetle instead.

You Know You're an MK when...

46. You stockpile mangoes.

47. You know what *real* coffee tastes like.

48. The majority of your friends never spoke English.

49. Someone brings up the name of a team, and you get the sport wrong.

50. You bundle up warmly, even in the middle of summer.

You Know You're an MK when...

51. You believe vehemently that football is played with a round, spotted ball.

52. A friend invites you to jam with him; he brings an electric guitar—you bring bongos.

53. You know there is no such thing as an international language.

54. You quote Reepicheep: Adventures are never fun while you're having them.

55. You know the difference between patriotism and nationalism.

56. You tell Americans that democracy isn't the only viable form of government.

57. You realize it really is a small world after all.

58. You never take anything for granted.

59. You feel a polka-dotted passport would be appropriate.

60. You watch a movie set in a foreign country, and you know what the nationals are *really* saying into the camera.

61. Rain on a tile patio — or a corrugated metal roof — is one of the most wonderful sounds in the world.

62. You know how to pack.

63. All preaching sounds better on hard, wooden benches.

64. A musical instrument can be anything— even a tambourine made from bottle caps nailed to a board.

65. Your roommate's stereo has ten times the wattage of your home church's PA system.

66. Fitting 15 or more people in a car seems normal to you.

67. You refer to gravel roads as highways.

You Know You're an MK when...

68. You haggle with the checkout clerk for a lower price.

69. You own appliances with three types of plugs, know the difference between 110 and 220 volts, 50 and 60 cycle current, and realize that a transformer isn't always enough to make your appliances work.

70. You fried a good number of appliances learning what you know in #69.

71. You marry another MK.

72. Your parents' siblings are strangers to you, but you have 50-60 Aunts and Uncles who are no blood relation to you at all.

73. You maintain a mailing list of over 400 names and addresses, but have no one you feel comfortable spending Christmas with.

74. You get upset when people don't finish their food, and feel worse when they scrape it into the trash.

75. You don't think that two hours is a long sermon.

76. There was never a special meal on Sunday, as it was your parents' busiest day. Monday was your Day of Rest.

77. You don't do well in job interviews because you were taught to be modest.

78. Your wardrobe can only handle two seasons: wet and dry.

79. You think nothing of straddling white lines to pass between trucks or buses traveling side by side, because, "There was plenty of room, officer. Honest! At least six inches clearance."

80. Someone in your passport country has to explain to you that the double yellow line means only oncoming traffic can drive on that side of the road, even when there isn't any oncoming traffic. ... and you don't understand why.

81. The same individual also has to explain that red lights mean stop, every time, without

exception, and you must stay stopped until they turn green, whether or not there is cross-traffic...and you still don't understand why.

82. Later the same day, the same poor friend has to go to great lengths to explain to you why you cannot just hand the policeman fifty cents and drive away when he stops you, and why you are now being driven downtown in the back of said officer's car over a mere fifty cents; at which point your passport country ceases to make any sense to you at all.

83. You can't get past "Oh, say can you see..." in the National Anthem, and you have to watch to see what hand to use.

84. You think the Pledge of Allegiance might possibly begin with "Fourscore and seven years ago...."

85. You get confused because dollar bills aren't color coded.

86. Your high school memories include those days that school was canceled due to tear gas.

You Know You're an MK when...

87. You listen to the latest hit on the radio and think "I wonder how that would sound on a thumb piano or a sitar?"

88. You feel odd being in the ethnic majority.

89. You go to the local Korean restaurant just to listen to the conversation.

90. You go to Taco Bell and have to put five packets of hot sauce on your taco before it seems even moderately spicy.

You Know You're an MK when...

91. You are accused by your friends of being a maniacal driver, and you're driving just like dad taught you to.

92. You have a hard time living with a roommate who isn't a foreigner.

93. You really do enjoy Oriental folk music.

94. Your family talks about "Grandpa Al," and you never met him before he died.

95. You marvel at the cleanliness of gas station bathrooms.

96. You instinctively start ripping up the newspaper when you run out of toilet paper.

97. The section on minor keys in music theory class makes you homesick.

98. You think you hear your mission country's language when you play a record backwards.

99. You miss the subtitles when you go to see the latest movie.

100. You feel like you need to move after you've lived in the same place for two months.

101. You eat a lot of chicken, because it tastes so similar to the dog meat that you miss.

102. You don't think of eating goldfish as an old fraternity prank.

103. You know what the name of your subcompact car means.

104. You know someone with the same name as your subcompact car.

105. You determine your speed by the smaller orange numbers on the inside of your speedometer dial.

106. You cruise the Internet looking for fonts that can support foreign alphabets.

107. Riots make you homesick.

108. You try to get onto a military base by showing your passport.

109. You have seen both the north star and the southern cross, and you can navigate by either constellation.

110. It scares you more to send your kids to public school than it would to send them on an unescorted plane trip.

111. You think VISA is a document stamped in your passport, not a plastic card you carry in your wallet.

112. You hear a song from the 50's and ask your friends who sings that new song.

113. All black people do not look even remotely alike, nor do all Hispanics or Asians... but Europeans and North Americans are kind of hard to tell apart at first.

114. Climates below 72° F (20° C) are against your body's religion.

115. The thought of encountering snakes, scorpions, wild animals, witch doctors or armed rebel insurgents on an afternoon walk evokes response like, "Yes...?" and "So...?" whereas the idea of driving through—let alone living in—an American city, terrifies you.

116. Someone asks you where you enjoy hanging out and you immediately think of the many hours happily spent in international airports.

117. In spite of your passport country's climate, your parent's influence, and your religious scruples, you have a total aversion to clothing more substantial than a thong bikini.

118. The thing that made you feel most at home when you returned to your passport country was the "new", "modern", body piercing and tattooing fad.

119.   You go to a church you have never been to before and find your picture on their bulletin board.

120.   The best word you can find to describe the U.S. is "fake".

121.   You find a gravel road, so you find some of your MK friends and go drive along it at night with the lights off and the windows down, reminiscing.

You Know You're an MK when...

122. The sole finally comes off your favorite pair of shoes, so you go looking for the itinerant shoe repair man who will fix 'em better than new, right there on the sidewalk while you wait.

123. Your idea of "we deliver" is buying fresh mangoes, pineapple, bananas, passion fruit, guavas—and other fruits that have no name in English—from the street vendor who comes by twice a day, knows exactly what kind of papaya you prefer, and always saves one out for you.

You Know You're an MK when...

124. You used to hate hand-me-down clothes, but when an old friend leaves a shirt at your place that happens to fit, you wear it often because it reminds you of your friend and your childhood.

125. You actually look forward to the rare times when the power goes off because you might get a chance to see the stars that are still etched so vividly in your memory.

126. You didn't get a license until your 18th birthday, but you started driving the ancient family Land Rover when you were seven, looking out through the raised ventilation louvers under the windshield.

127. For years, you thought those ventilation louvers were what air-conditioning meant.

128. You have this deep, sinking feeling that someone, somewhere, has that fifth grade braces-and-stringy-hair picture of you on their refrigerator.

You Know You're an MK when...

129. You look at the Rockies and think, "Nice hills."

130. You automatically take off your shoes as soon as you get home.

131. You visit an Ancient History museum and see a display of tools and household implements that you have used often and may even still own.

132. Your living room looks like a little museum with all the "exotic" things you have around.

133. You know hundreds of missionaries all over the world, but forget your pastor's name.

134. You consider a three year-old piece of clothing to be practically new.

135. You get nostalgic about sleeping every night in the summer under mosquito netting, after the bed has been dusted with DDT and the air sprayed with Flit, and little green spirally things are burning in every room of the house.

You Know You're an MK when...

136. You don't know whether to write the date as month/day/year, day/month/year, or some variation thereof.

137. You play tricks with the International Date Line.

138. You meet another MK, and discover that you share the same best friend.

139. The best word for something is the word you learned first, and you still use those words, even if you now know what they are in English.

140. The place you call home no longer exists.

141. All your life, you knew you could get home just by walking towards the mountains... until you visited Iowa, that is, and got horribly lost.

142. You mesclar your idiomas without thinking about it.

143. You embarrass yourself publicly by automatically picking up and using what turn out to be not-so-palatable expressions.

144. You won't eat Uncle Ben's rice because it doesn't stick together.

145. Your friends nervously remind you to drive on the right side of the road.

146. You get mad at minorities complaining of discrimination when they have no clue as to what it's like to be a real minority.

147. Half of your phone calls are unintelligible to those around you.

148. You occasionally feel an urge to climb a volcano, but can't find one.

149. You wake up one day and realize you're not a foreigner anymore.

150. You wake up on a different day and realize you really still are a foreigner.

151. When traveling around the world, you feel at home in other countries even though you haven't lived there.

152. Even at distant international airports, you're always running into people you know.

153. You grow up thinking you're really tall for your age.

154. Your parents ask you what certain words mean.

155. Your best friends live thousands of miles away.

156. The first thing you ask your parents on the phone is "What time is it?"

157. You enjoy speaking a foreign language with a bad accent when you are with your friends to mock the pronunciation of other foreigners.

158. You want to write "MK" in the "other" box under ethnic origin.

159. When you were younger, you thought your dad wrote letters for his job.

160. You still feel the urge to fill the tub when the electricity goes off, because you know the water is next.

161. You honk your horn at an intersection to let people know you're coming through and everyone gives you looks that could kill.

162. You go into withdrawal because you don't get time off for your "home" country's holidays, such as Cinco de Mayo, Chinese New Year, etc.

163. You think commercials are the best part of watching TV.

164. Seeing a shriveled-up mango in the grocery store makes you yearn for the real thing, along with other tropical fruits that are unknown to the Western palate.

165. All the other freshmen at college are homesick, can't do their own laundry, won't try new things, and you want to tell them to grow up!

166. You dream in a foreign language.

167. You still hesitate before drinking water straight from the tap.

168. You never know what to say when asked for a "permanent address."

169. You raise sheep, learn line dancing, or go skydiving just to have an excuse to be weird.

You Know You're an MK when...

170. You're amazed to learn that a strike, a picket line, and a riot are all different things.

171. You re-wash all your plastic bags and refold tinfoil for future use.

172. You can quote you parents' sermons from furlough word for word.

173. You have a traditional wedding—traditional Colombian outfits for the men, traditional Indian outfits for the women, traditional vows from Afghanistan, all held in a traditional North American church.

You Know You're an MK when...

174. You know that they don't speak Mexican in Mexico.

175. Your phone bill is as much as your car payment.

176. Friends wonder why you're never in the same church twice.

177. When riding your bike, you watch out for wildlife, not cars.

178. Your idea of good accommodations is the Motel 6 right off the interstate.

179. You measure distance in time, and time in days.

180. You know a smattering of more foreign languages than you can remember, but cannot fully express yourself in any of them.

181. No matter where you are in the world, you don't feel as if you belong, and vehemently defend the fact that you don't.

182. You occasionally feel a cultural barrier between you and those who raised you, and have no idea what to do about it.

183. You're sitting somewhere, in the middle of middle-class suburbia, and a seemingly random word sets your mind off over time and space, and leaves you devastated at the fact that you were where you were, and that you could never go back to what you had.

184. You've ever cried in a computer lab.

185. Old ladies you don't know say, "I used to change your diapers."

186. You ask where Michael Jackson's other glove is.

You Know You're an MK when...

187.   You realize that the Spanish word that was okay in Ecuador is not okay in Mexico.

189.   You bow when talking on the phone.

190.   Going to the post office is the highlight of your day.

191.   You have red hair, and are constantly pestered by people who "just want to touch it."

192.   After a church service, you look for a slide projector to put away.

193. You asked Santa for a Butterfinger, and told your grandmother you wanted Band-Aids and Scotch tape for Christmas.

194. You carry Bibles in two languages to church.

195. You watch an English language movie and read the foreign language subtitles.

196. You send out wedding invitations in more than one language.

197. You carry a dictionary everywhere you go.

You Know You're an MK when...

198. At five feet tall, your mother is taller than most of your church members.

199. Adults want to pay you to teach them English.

200. You can't find shoes to fit your feet in any of the shoe stores.

201. Home is where you hang your hammock.

202. Your native friends ask if you know Michael Jordan.

203. Your family gathers around the computer to check the E-mail.

204. At your yard sale, an 80 year old man buys your mother's culottes.

205. Your native friends know more English grammar than you do, but can't understand English conversation.

206. You have carried the same dollar bill in your wallet for years.

207. You watch the Super Bowl live on Monday morning.

208. The traffic light turns from red to blue.

209. You find eating spaghetti with chopsticks easier than using a fork and spoon.

210. You are thankful for running hot water.

211. Kerosene lamps make you homesick.

212. You spend hours walking down the aisles of a grocery store without buying anything.

You Know You're an MK when...

213. You were given a map of the US to fill in, and marked several places "Destroyed by nuclear bombs" just to fill all that white space.

214. You consider parasites, dysentery, or tropical diseases to be appropriate dinner conversation.

215. You consider it normal to have the above-mentioned illnesses.

216. You tell people what certain gestures mean in different parts of the world.

You Know You're an MK when...

217. You have stopped in the middle of an argument to find the translation of a word you just used.

218. You calculate exchange rates by the price of Coke.

219. You pronounce Z as "zed," just to irritate Americans.

220. You thought the movie "The Gods Must Be Crazy" was too realistic to be funny.

221. You enjoy textual criticism of customs forms.

222. Every three years you get an irresistible urge to move to a different country.

223. You think living in one place all your life is exotic.

224. You go to McDonald's and take home the extra ketchup and sugar packages.

225. You're amazed at how empty US city buses are.

226. It feels weird to stop at a "rest stop" instead of using the bush.

227. All of your clothes have name labels. Sometimes they even have your own name.

228. You eat all of the food on your plate, and, after rinsing it off, the food that fell on the ground, as well.

229. You know the current news of nine other countries, but know nothing about what's going on in the States.

230. During furlough, you wake up in the morning and ask your Mom what state you are in.

231. You can't figure out how American super-markets can offer fresh produce in the middle of winter.

232. A total stranger says you stayed at his house for three weeks when you were five.

233. You argue with your parents over how you dress, and you protest that all the other kids your age wear loincloths, too.

234. You know not to joke around at border crossings.

You Know You're an MK when...

235. You wonder how Americans dare question the virtues of their governmental policies.

236. You answer "Yes" to the question: "Where have you lived all your life—some desert island?"

237. You say something—not entirely divine— and your friend says, "I thought you were a missionary kid!"

238. You tell time using a 24 hour clock.

239. You'd rather sleep on the floor than on a soft mattress.

You Know You're an MK when...

240. Your address book is thicker than your dictionary.

241. Snow and automatic transmissions are things you've heard of, but never actually seen.

242. You know you aren't going to move for a while when your parents throw out the packing boxes.

243. You still listen carefully for a dial tone before you dial a number.

244. You preferred powdered milk to the "real" stuff.

245. You show up at the cafeteria carrying hot salsa, fish sauce, marmite and any number of other essentials from home.

246. Your amazement with the softness of American toilet paper is only second to your amazement that it actually tears at the perforations.

247. You get frustrated with store clerks who know nothing about PAL VCRs.

248. You try to find VOA (Voice of America) frequencies in the USA.

You Know You're an MK when...

249. You put ice in milk, and drink soda at room temperature.

250. You ask, "US Dollars?" when someone in the US gives you a price.

251. People keep Fido away from you when they learn what used to supplement your diet.

252. People leave the table when you start telling stories of things you have eaten while on the field.

You Know You're an MK when...

253. Your high school friends are now spread out all over the world.

254. You get frustrated when other people tell you how the world should be run.

255. You buy rice in bulk.

256. You eat with chopsticks.

257. You eat with your fingers.

258. You eat everything with a knife and fork, including pizza and oranges.

259. The goodbyes make your high school grad-
uation is the saddest day of your life.

260. You went to grade school on one continent,
high school on another, and college on a third.

261. You first get to the mission field, and you
don't drink the coffee because it has bugs in
it. After a year or so, you go ahead and drink
the coffee, even though you know very well
that it has bugs in it. Years later, you return to
the States, and are very suspicious of the
coffee, because it doesn't have bugs in it.

You Know You're an MK when...

262. You don't remember who the President of the United States is but can name the leader(s) of almost any other country.

263. You slip into another language when you're mad.

264. You have Sunday school in your bedroom, church in your kitchen, and the offering plate gets washed with the lunch dishes.

265. You have to make a conscious effort not to kiss Americans when you greet them.

266. You believe that, to be able to converse in several languages is valuable, but to be able to hold your tongue in one is priceless.

267. You almost start to cry in the import section of the grocery store—and even then, you can't find monkey meat, groundhog, or bush rat.

268. You think of yourself as Norwegian when you're in Papua New Guinea, Papua New Guinean when you're in the US, and American when you're in Norway.

269. You put money in your socks instead of your wallet, and have a supply of cold, hard cash in your freezer.

270. You have late night meals consisting of Japanese noodles, Indian chai, Malaysian guava juice, Swedish cookies, and Norwegian cripsbread with German Nutella, topped off with some strong PNG style coffee.

271. You buy tinned fish with rice even though you hate it—just for old times' sake.

You Know You're an MK when...

272. You use only half the bag of chocolate chips when making a double recipe of cookies.

273. You ask the checkout clerk at K-Mart how she is, how her family is, how her garden is, how her cows are...

274. You get excited about ice cream, but think that Baskin & Robbins might be a legal firm, Hägen Daas a European conductor, and TCBY a mission organization (Taking Christ's Blessing to Youth).

You Know You're an MK when...

275.   You watch *The Simpsons* to find out what Americans are like.

276.   You find yourself collecting the familiar stickers off of the tropical fruits you buy at the grocery store.

277.   After you tell someone where you're from, they reply "My, your English is very good." and you want to respond, "Why, thank you. So is yours."

278. You keep pictures of your parents displayed around the house so your kids will know who their other grandparents are.

279. You've already had more than four years' experience in dorm pranks before you ever get to college.

280. You have never called a 1-800 number in your life.

281. You take it for granted that you get to go first in line at the missions conference potluck.

You Know You're an MK when...

282. Your cold cereal comes with instructions on how to eat it.

283. You still occasionally miss the toys that you had to give away when you moved.

284. You drive two hours to go to a McDonald's.

285. None of your neighbors can pronounce the name of your dog.

286. You go to pick the beautiful flowers in the yard... and someone informs you that they're weeds.

287. College students ask you to help them with their English homework.

288. You mail people birthday cards two months before their birthday.

289. You have ever seen an adult buy and eat a Happy Meal at McDonald's.

290. You wonder why American coins don't have pictures of royalty on them.

291. You have ever been excited to get a two-year old Reader's Digest.

You Know You're an MK when...

292. You eat at someone's house, and you don't ask what was in the meal until after you are done.

293. You have often had to insist that you only have one last name.

294. You have gone to church Sunday morning in one state and Sunday evening in another.

295. You can convert Celsius to Fahrenheit on your fingers.

296. Kool-Aid is worth its weight in gold to you.

You Know You're an MK when...

297. All the dictionaries in your house are bilingual.

298. You think wearing Levi's is a status symbol.

299. You get Christmas packages on Valentine's day.

300. You are relieved on furlough that all the old ladies don't kiss you.

301. You have brown hair and people say "Look at the blond American!"

302. You go "home" on furlough and get homesick.

You Know You're an MK when...

303. You've heard too many people ask, "Which do you like better, this country or the other one?"

304. You live in a city of over a million people and there are no drive-up windows.

305. You have seen more bull fights on TV than baseball games.

306. You view laws as helpful guidelines that need interpretation depending on the situation.

307. You've been married for more than 20 years before you show your spouse where you grew up.

308. You've heard "People Need the Lord" more times and in more languages than Steve Green... who is an MK himself.

309. You teach children's church in two languages; neither of which is the mother tongue of anyone present.

310. People always put your country of birth in the wrong continent.

311. You were "officially" taught that there are 5, 6, or even 7 continents, depending on the teacher.

312. Your alphabets don't have 26 letters.

313. You can't comfortably type on a QWERTY keyboard.

314. You ask who the current prime minister of the U.S. is.

315. You have legitimate claims to two or more passports.

316. You're the only one who knows the postal rates to each continent without looking it up.

317. Your telephone's autodialer can't store enough digits for each phone number.

318. You have to translate government forms for embassy staff.

319. You have a cross stitch sampler that says, "Dorm, sweet dorm."

320. You ask your host if they flush after each use.

321. You leave a store at noon expecting they will close for lunch and siesta.

322. You frequently miscount bank notes as 25s instead of 20s, and have trouble remembering how much nickels and dimes are worth.

323. You request a third world roommate in college because the rest of the students are strange.

324. Someone mentions a Rogue's Gallery, and you ask who Rogue was, and what kind of art he collected.

325. You have had your pets stolen and eaten.

326. You think someone is drunk when they are driving in a straight line, instead of swerving to miss the potholes.

327. Every time you go to a store in the US you buy rare items like chocolate chips in cases because they may not be there next time.

328. You leave the lights on all night—just because you can.

329. You're going to Grandma's house in Ohio, so you round up roller bandages, sandwiches and water, and fill up the gasoline container.

330. You go a day without eating rice and feel like you haven't eaten.

331. You experience a breathless, wild excitement whenever your speedometer hits 45 m.p.h.

332. You hear people complaining about potholes in the roads, and you can't see any.

333. You keep checking the electric refrigerator to see if it needs more kerosene.

334. You can come up with a substitute for any —or even all—the ingredients in a recipe.

335. People assume that you lived in constant danger, surrounded by savage, naked cannibals on a desert island, where you lived in a mud hut and rode a donkey to school.

336. You have a built-in ability to create what you need from what you already have.

You Know You're an MK when...

337. Your cheeks are sore from being pinched and told "My, how you've grown!"

338. You tell the clerk at the shoe store that your shoe size is 38... and you don't know why he laughed so much.

339. You're accustomed to homemade peppermint ice cream being cement gray from the mix of the green and red peppermint sticks that were added to it for flavor.

340. You consider furniture purchases based on how sturdy, movable or easily dismantled they are.

341. You're used to calculating money in six digits.

342. You think the list of "childhood diseases" includes amebic dysentery, stomach worms, and malaria.

343. The first time you spoke to your grandmother you called her "auntie".

344. You call senior missionaries "grandma and grandpa."

345. Your understanding of "fast food" is a quick chicken.

You Know You're an MK when...

346. The phrase, "going home" means one thing to your parents, and a different thing to you.

347. The message on your answering machine is in two languages.

348. Earthquakes are normal, daily events.

349. Your Mom sends you out to sweep the street in front of your house.

350. You pull into a gas station and expect people to come running out yelling, "Welcome!"

351. Your class ranking is one of two options.

352. You know what kind of underwear all your boarding school classmates wear.

353. You have a whole collection of signs that were written in hilarious attempts at English.

354. You hear "Love Offering" and think about how you'll spend the money.

355. You walk down the street and pick up shattered glass so that people won't cut their feet.

You Know You're an MK when...

356. Drinking a Coke from a can is a special treat.

357. The sibling you grew up with has a totally different accent from you.

358. You're 25 before you realize that you don't have to buy everything secondhand.

359. In the US, you get a strange feeling because there is no one walking down the street.

360. Your hand-me-downs are the new fashion— and you look hip, but you feel awful.

You Know You're an MK when...

361. People say, "Say something!" but it isn't because you've fainted— they just want to hear the way you speak.

362. You say you're sorry for everything, regardless of whether it is your fault or not.

363. People don't understand that you can be from Africa and still be white.

364. You don't know how to make Hungry Jack pancakes, and wish you could just make them from scratch.

You Know You're an MK when...

365. You could easily fall asleep while traveling on a rutted, gravel road.

366. You know about 30 different ways of asking for a bathroom break.

367. You can't find all the letters or symbols you need on your keyboard.

368. A burst of static on the phone makes you proclaim, "That's what I said, OVER!"

369. You get lost in Wal-Mart.

370. You think that nude/topless bathing isn't all that uncommon.

371. You complain when an international newspaper only has half a page devoted to non-US news.

372. You claim no place as home, but you do home-schooling.

373. Your grandparents actually wish you were around more often.

374. TV seems juvenile and boring.

375. No pizza parlor concoction can beat your own home-cooked sauerkraut pizza.

376. Your American friends seem to have strange eating habits.

377. You are anxious for furlough to end so that life can get back to normal.

378. You understand the concept of infinity—it is the time between letters.

379. You really do believe in miracles.

You Know You're an MK when...

380. Before you were even ten, you traveled alone, understood terms like customs and immigration, and knew exactly how many kilos you could pack into a suitcase and get away with it.

381. A 54 hour train ride doesn't seem like such a long time.

382. For fun, you try to see how many people you can fit into a trolley-bus.

383. A washing machine is a luxury.

You Know You're an MK when...

384. You tell people where you're from and have to spend the next half hour explaining where that is.

385. You can fly home free on Frequent Flyer miles.

386. You have no problem with global warming.

387. You fly home for Christmas, spend 26 hours on a plane, and arrive the same day you left.

388. You have strong opinions about public transportation.

389. You know how to avoid jet-lag.

390. You keep up with foreign exchange rates.

391. The phrase: "Act your age and not your shoe size!" doesn't mean what you think it does.

392. You grow up thinking you'll become a linguist or a translator.

393. The prospect of dying for your faith is much easier to grasp than being ridiculed for your clothes.

You Know You're an MK when...

394. You resent having to wear shoes to school.

395. You go camping in the US and the bathroom facilities are better than those you had at home while growing up.

396. You know the difference between socialism and communism.

397. You get marriage proposals from nationals who see you as a walking green card.

398. You try to explain the existence of unseen things, such as God, microbes, and airplane propellers.

399. You've never seen Star Wars.

400. You call a friend for 20 minutes and end up paying over $60 for that one phone call.

401. You can recognize a faked accent.

402. You have seen most of the seven natural and man-made wonders of the world.

403. You eat to live instead of living to eat.

404. You ground yourself before you pick up the phone.

405. You can negotiate with a phone operator in any language.

406. You listen to shortwave radio instead of watching TV.

407. You can convince your friends that you know five different languages when you actually only know three.

408. You realize that they will believe just about anything you say, as long as it's weird enough.

409. You go to Pier 1 Imports and wonder why they're charging so much money for such ordinary things.

410. You are introduced to someone, and, instead of the expected kiss, to your horror, you are bear hugged and pounded on the back.

411. You miss being able to see the stars.

412. You have to tell the travel agent the three-letter airport code for the destination you're traveling to, andwhat connections you will needto make, and what airlines fly there.

413. You can't understand why people are so upset when you're 15 minutes late.

414. You try to sack your own groceries at the grocery store.

415. You're the only one not complaining that the weather forecast is "snow."

416. You'd rather be hot than cold.

417. You'd rather be barefoot.

418. The opulence of padded pews and choir robes makes you furious.

You Know You're an MK when...

419. Your host in your passport country catches you admiring the way the salt flows freely from the salt shaker.

420. You gain 30 pounds every time you go to the U.S.

421. You have no idea who Rush Limbaugh, Dave Letterman, Newt Gingrich, Jay Leno, and Bob Dole are.

422. Your all-time favorite movie is "The Gods Must be Crazy."

You Know You're an MK when...

423. People in America have never even heard of your favorite meal.

424. You shudder at the amount of makeup used by high school girls.

425. You prefer to ride on top of the car instead of inside it.

426. You laugh at the different hairstyles around.

427. Your first impression of Americans is that they are so white and fat.

You Know You're an MK when...

428. You think sugar is the favorite American spice.

429. You cough and gag in church in the States because of all the hair spray and perfume, and wish for some good ol' B.O.

430. You bravely face down and kill a garter snake.

431. Other kids' grubby clothes look like your best ones.

432. You know what "roughing it" really is.

433. You get lost in the cities because every street looks the same.

You Know You're an MK when...

434. You wear sandals until the first snowfall.

435. You like boiled sugar-water and maple flavoring better than extra rich maple syrup.

436. In the US on furlough, you accidentally speak to darker skinned Americans in your other language.

437. You wanted to play "border-crossing" and "travel agent" instead of "cowboys and Indians" with your Stateside cousins.

You Know You're an MK when...

438. You wondered about exchange rates before most kids knew that the dollar wasn't the only currency.

439. You take a secret delight in seeing the US trampled in world competition by any small insignificant country.

440. The cashier in the grocery store asks, "Paper or plastic?" and you reply, "I'll be paying in cash."

441. "Getting your shots" means being vaccinated painfully for deadly diseases every six months or so.

You Know You're an MK when...

442. Sometimes you wonder if it is worth it— but you've seen people die from those diseases.

443. You remember the glass syringes and dull, shared needles with questionable sterilization procedures.

444. You've been to a dentist with the foot pedal and pulley drill system.

445. You listen carefully to the list of diseases they ask you about when you give blood because you've had a couple of them.

446. You've seen and known actual leprosy patients.

447. You know the bitter taste of antimalarial quinine pills.

448. You used to hate taking quinine pills, but now tonic water is one of your favorite drinks because the quinine taste brings back fond memories.

449. You find your fresh fruit tastes strange if it hasn't been soaked in an iodine solution for at least 15 minutes.

You Know You're an MK when...

450. Every time you smell Clorox you think of fresh vegetables.

451. You still shake your boots out every morning.

452. You feel sorry for peers who did not grow up overseas or go to boarding school.

453. You describe Americans as if you were not one yourself.

454. You rate girls on the basis of their ability to eat hot curry.

455. The only all 4.0 semester you got in college was when you took four semesters' worth of foreign language in one semester to fulfill the foreign language requirement.

456. You recognize that Jabba the Hut (from Star Wars) is really speaking Kikuyu, the language spoken around Nairobi, Kenya.

457. You wish for real sugar instead of that white, wimpy stuff they use in the US.

458. Nationals think your Dad works for the CIA.

You Know You're an MK when...

459. Your friends wonder why you're in the restaurant washroom so long and find you swapping jokes with the Spanish-speaking attendant.

460. You still do your math in another language.

461. You can read the manuals for your television and VCR.

462. You were baptized in a bathtub.

463. Your parents teach you English and you teach them Japanese.

464. You verify the nationality of a restaurant owner before eating there.

465. You call gravy "sauce."

466. All your life, you have been defined by your parents profession, and now you want an identity of your own.

467. If you had to flee the country, and could only take two things, you know what you would take—because you have had to.

You Know You're an MK when...

468. Your parents have converted and discipled hundreds of other people, but your own faith is shrouded in doubt.

469. You felt that you were sent to boarding school so your parents would have more time to work.

470. You tell the teacher you are from Timbuktu, and she sends you to the principal's office for being sassy.

471. Witnessing in English just doesn't seem natural.

472. "Weather forecasting" means looking across the valley at the approaching wall of rain and knowing you have less than five minutes to get the clothes off the line.

473. You are heartbroken about a plane crash half a world away in a country you do not know.

474. The most dreaded form of torture imaginable is to be stood up in front of a class an asked to name the capitals of all 50 states.

475. Tentacles in your food don't bother you.

You Know You're an MK when...

476. You argue at length about whether or not to cross your sevens.

477. People often find you whistling, "Anywhere I Hang My Hat is Home."

478. You married an American and think it is one of the most interesting things you have experienced so far.

479. Visitors come from the US, and you ask them to bring you lime Jell-O and graham crackers.

▌▐▌

You Know You're an MK when...

480. Americans see your home town as a tourist spot.

481. You talk in your sleep, but it's not in English.

482. You've never seen "Gilligan's Island."

483. You sweep a carpeted floor with a broom.

484. You think "Red Hot Chili Peppers" is a snack, not a band.

485. The book of Job haunts you to this day.

You Know You're an MK when...

486. You remember playing one-man Frisbee with the typhoons.

487. Upon your first encounter with an automatic door, you ran back to your mother and said, "Look, mommy, I scared those doors open!"

488. Apples are a rare treat, but papayas are normal.

489. The road sign says "bump," and five miles down the road, you become curious, as you haven't felt anything.

You Know You're an MK when...

490. People simply don't understand.

491. You are singled out in Sunday School class to speak about "your country."

492. You pretend not to know your "other" language when it is convenient.

493. You feel guilty if you own anything new.

494. Your puns cross three languages.

495. You can recognize another MK in a crowd.

You Know You're an MK when...

496. Some of your happiest childhood memories involved playing in packing boxes and old barrels.

497. You long for letters, but can never write them.

498. You know it is possible to laugh and cry at the same time.

499. The most precious friend you have is the one that promises never to leave you or forsake you.

500. Heaven is the only place you can call home.

There's no way we could have done this book alone. A BIG thank you to the following contributors:

Joel Jackson, Beth Gualtieri Goff, Mimi Barker, Jennifer Ostini, Ibancorp, Dorothy Haines, Chris Peterson, Katy, Rachel Burney, Edwin and Carolyn Kerr, Nate Hekman, Joe McDonald, Ginna Scott, Debi Johnson, Melody Faris, Iain Wilson, Todd Bushong, "Andrew", Dan Erickson; Joy, Ronnie, and Mary Hudson, Jen Curry, "Christopher", Elisabeth Cameron, V.J. Giles, Laura Vaughn, Daniel Ruhkala, Michail Chaigne, John "Tommy" Tompkins, Bobby Ellis, Lauren Bisset, Heidi Evensen, Liz Meiners, John P. Cardoza, Paul Renaud, Benjamin "Scotty" Wisley, Mike and Anna Hilton, Joan Myers, Danny Plett, Adelle Horst Ward, Chuck Roswell, Pam Giles, Donna (Cole) Carter, Jeff Carter, John Connor, Paul D. Hefft, Kirsten Olguin, Teresa Weide, Philip Burgess, Ana R. Mann, Harold and Carolyn Curtis, Esly Regina Carvalho, Chris LaTondresse, Nadia Fischer, Nathan Hammond, Laurie Connolly, Jack W. Elliston, Natalie Maldonado, Veronika Oleksyn, Gary M. Ruba, "Tyler", Duane Moyer, Angel S. Hines, Pat Doty, Nathaniel Scott Waldock, Chris Gage,

Rebecca Jacob, Dave Aufrance, Trevor Nelson, Sandi Wistley, Erik Mugele, Rick Rineer, "MAC", Jamie Reed, Jennifer Brizendene, Rachel O'Dell, Don Van Den Berg, Reenie (Corey) Posey, Amy Keith ...and everybody else on the planet in case I missed somebody.

Extra Special thanks go to Nate Hekman, Mimi Barker, Donna Carter, Susan Hands, Iain C. Wilson, Beth Goff and Paul Spite for all of your technical help, advice and encouragement.

Thanks, Leo and Jeff, for putting up with us through the whole production, and making this whole thing a reality. Thanks to Andy, Jentesal, Jonadab, Sara, Sarah, Bethany, Tony, Mark, Mom, Dad, Martha and anyone else who helped us with collating and assembly. (Are we *done* yet?)

Ultimate praise goes to God, for putting us in this position in the first place.

Enjoy! May God bless you.

—Andy and Deborah

Ordering Information

Want your own copy? Want to give one as a gift? It's easy!
Price per book:* $5.00
Shipping and Handling: 1–6 books / $3.00; 7–10 books / $4.00;
11-15 books / $6.00   *For larger orders, please contact us.*
Canadian customers add $1; Outside US and Canada, add $2.

Please make checks or money orders payable to Andy and Deborah Kerr, and made out in US funds. Books will be shipped upon receipt of payment.

> MK List
> 307 Administration Boulevard
> Winona Lake, IN 46590
> USA

*Bulk pricing is available for orders of 20 books or more. Contact us for information.
*If this book is more than two years old, you can send e-mail to **mk@cheerful.com** for updated*
*information. Visit our new website at **http://www.mklist.com** for this and other MK-related*
*books. The Kerrs can be contacted at the above address, by e-mail at **kerr@kconline.com**,*
*or through their website at **http://www.members.kconline.com/kerr** .*

Order Form

Name _____

Address _____

City, State, Zip _____

Country _____ Daytime Phone (___) ___ - _____

Email Address _____

_____ Books at \$5 each... _____

Shipping and Handling (See previous page)... _____

IN Residents add 5% Sales Tax... _____

TOTAL _____

_____
Authorizing Signature (for Credit Card Orders)

(Circle one) **MC / VISA / Check**

Credit Card Number (please give entire number)

		•		

Expiration Date